boys.

poetry,
photography,
and artwork by boy blue.

1st Edition.

cover design by Verónica González

ISBN 978-1-7366239-1-6 (Hardcover)
ISBN 978-1-7366239-0-9 (Paperback)

https://boyblue.works

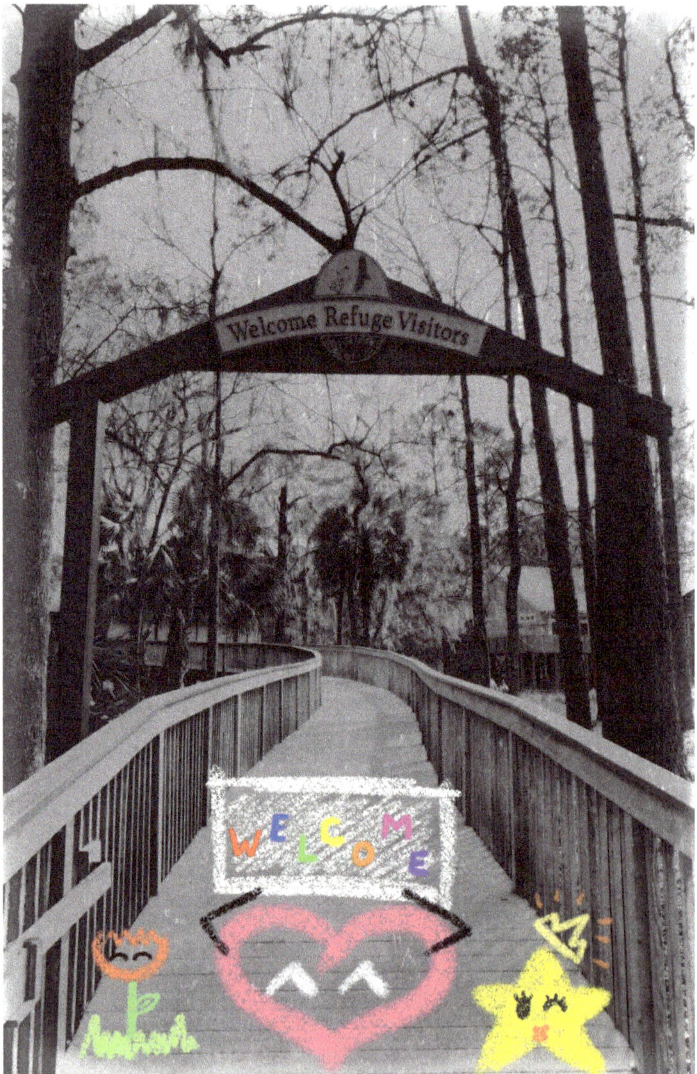
Welcome Refuge Visitors
WELCOME

CHAPTERS:

intro.

it's amusing to me that i titled this collection "boys." when the guys i talk about here are all men. "boys" just sounds better than "guys" or "men" though, don't you think? to be honest, although these boys are all grown up, the title comes from a place of nostalgia for an inspired guy who was experiencing severe peter pan syndrome so go along with it, I beg!

first, some backstory:
i had never really dated until i reached my twenties.
it was strange for me to start a journey late in life that everyone around me had already been on.
i'd find myself meeting a person and writing a hundred poems about their hair or the ways they made mine raise.

pretty people poetry. stranger serenades.
odes to one-night stands.

i had no word or knowledge for the emotions i had, for the ones that were fleeting or for the ones that lingered. passion can be felt in different flavors, several shapes, varying lengths, but still have only one name: love.
Does it ever make you wonder if there are more dimensions to love than the forever one we all know about?

some might call these love poems.
who's to say.
can one meet, love, and let go in a day?
what i do know, though, is that if i am going to love,

i am going to do so unconditionally.
and i know that it means that if i am going to hurt,
i will do so wholeheartedly.
the balance of life.
it gives, it takes.
it's a risk i never look back on.

"boys." is a collection of poems that marked the start of my dating odyssey. these poems are chronicles of how i felt for a few of those boys. totally recommend. it's got everything you want from a story except it's not a story, it's poems! mysterious men, explicit behavior, budding romance, summer flings, elusive closures, and even some who got away, ooo.
(note: every chapter was written, beginning to end, during my time with said person)

i wrote these thoughts down and put line breaks in between them because they look prettier that way, but mostly because i had no more space inside to store the emotion and it spilled it's way onto paper. i hope that those who love in excess can find respite in these words.

my poetry collections are chapters of me, and "boys." archives the mature sentiments i had about a boyish time in my life. i finished this collection once i started finding my way and no longer felt like a boy anymore.

thank you for reading, you have no idea how happy you've made the boy who wrote this.

this is for you,
baby boy blue.

remember when you thought
no one would love you?

when you thought
this was something you couldn't do?

here's to always finding you untrue.

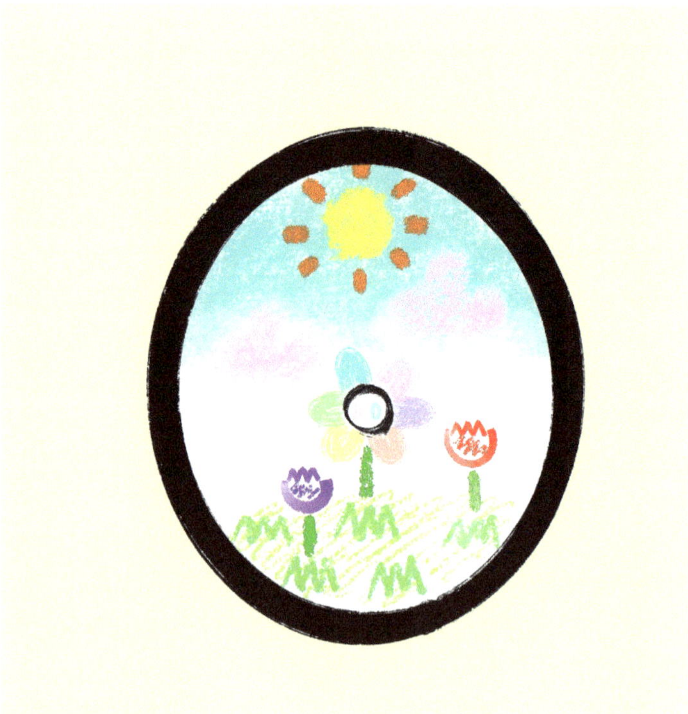

one
two
three
four

i declare a boy war

five
six
seven
eight

which one's worth the wait?

henry

i like boys of all ages, and you just so happened to be
21 years older than me.

tall, dark, and handsome with a matching tank top,
driving around in your big truck, smiling nonstop.
we always spent our nights together in different hotel rooms,
you'd show me old films and cook some gourmet food

but you had a lot of rough edges, a lot to hide
it followed you around sometimes, a few years done for crime
maybe some other time,
under better circumstances, we would have had a better chance...
but here's a few poems about our little dance in romance-

untitled.62818

we watched a movie, it was alright
well you did, i watched you all night
the way you clap with so much slap...

you smile at me like you always do,
just draw me a map to the rest of you.

Sir Noir

the brush of a touch on piano keys
as low and bittersweet as the times you leave
melody plays as you walk away
i follow the rise and fall of your chest like I count the seconds that you rest

i've got your Prince album in my car
50 miles apart but the CD player's never far
like the sounds of glass on the table of a sports bar
or when you snore next to me on the beach's boulevard

longing gazes in our shower hazes
housekeeping knows us by name
two fools diving in bottomless pools
in countless hotel rooms, none one and the same.

peace and blessings, count your endings.
your voicemail is full of what exactly?
broken hearted cries for a reply?
you say "just ask me" but say it so abstractly

you have the mystery of a murder noir
everything in plain sight but it's all in black and white.
crime scene blues with jazzy hues
chalk outline somewhere between wrong and right

untitled.71918

i'm the snap of a band that
got stretched out of hand

i'm the silence of a room
that's too alive to be a tomb

i'm the friction of rope
that's held too long to hope

i'm the tension in the thread
between his home and your bed.

When you said "nothing compares to you",

did you mean I'm better than or equal to?

untitled.72118

lotta texts, no replies
just a long list of alibis

lotta "what's this" and "I try"s
so now i'm wondering why

young, dumb, with a lot of time to waste
hung, wrung, and starving for a taste
eager to please, i'll set you at ease
but please do tell what's in it for me?

white beard, black truck
so cute, you got me stuck
but a derelict past that's forced to last
too old to hope, broke as a joke
emotional mess (and no sex)
with you, i never know what's next

i think our time has run its course, and
you know what they say about closed doors...

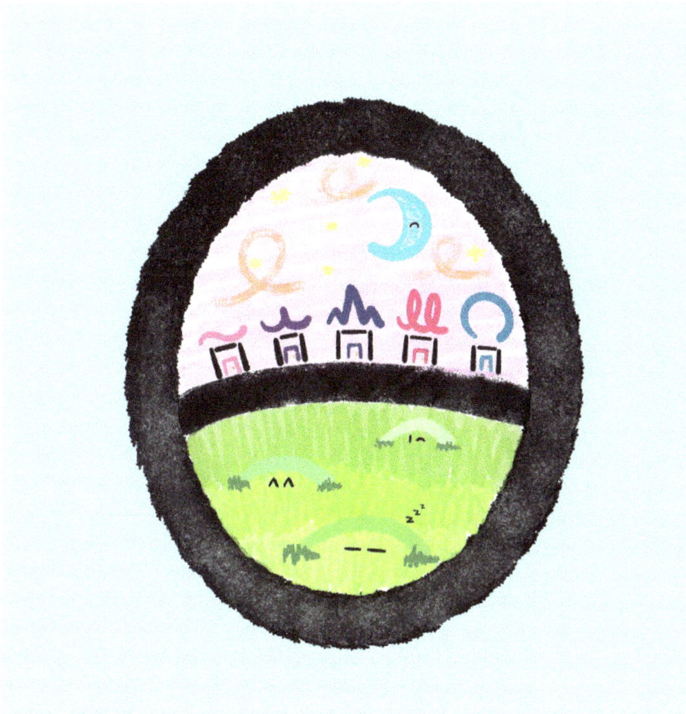

aj

i often wonder what would have been if
you hadn't walked my way.
what if we had stayed a summer fling?

can you believe we met organically?
asked a friend "who's that" one day
and we ended up moving to Tallahassee

i loved you during sweetener
left you with thank u, next
i couldn't hear positions without sending you a text

i'm sorry i left you with nothing to show,
you gave me so much to say
and now I'm just a lesson to know

Starlight

i met you out on the town one night
a candlelight in a raging riot
out of sight out of mind
but it wasn't long until you left me blind

you invited me in, heard me out
you opened your heart and showed me around
young and sound
at an age i was far from found

i saw your vinyl collection
there's some connection in your vintage selection
about 30 strong, some opened real long
and i added 19 to complete all her songs...

untitled.91018

moon to your night, sun to my day
the tide shifts to take my breath away
and today, if i may, i'll just lie here and stay
thinking about how you look at me that way.
what can i say,
i knew you were bae when you said
you read The Picture of Dorian Gray.

but you had me at hey anyway.

it's been so long since I've been drawn to write,

could you stand still so I could type the light right?

untitled.8218

i want to paint in the color of you
color my world in the hue of you
could you be pink or baby blue?
i want to discover every shade of you

i want to make my bed in your head
what makes you tick? makes you blush red?
would i find something dark instead,
tucked under the covers of your bedspread?

i want to build a home in the depths of you
find solace alone in every breath of you
i'll make our castle leagues under your sea
and sing you a song under the weight of me.

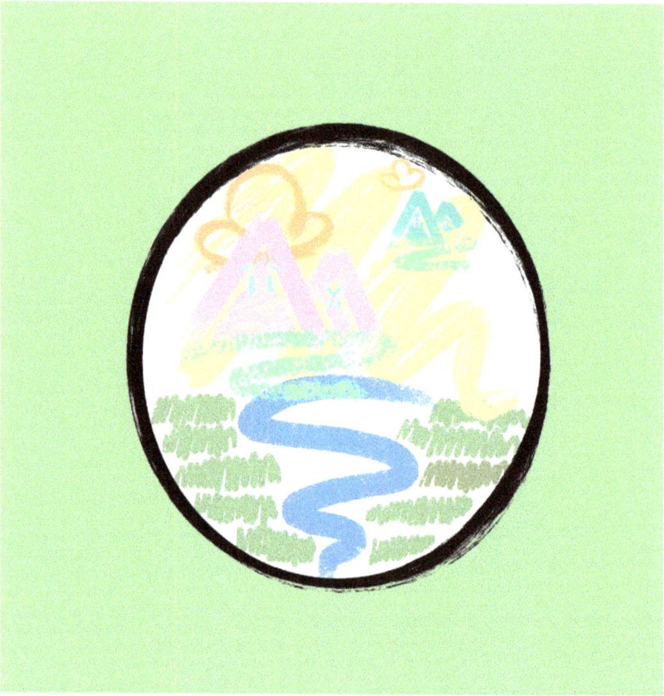

untitled.8118

hear ye, hear me

surprise surprise
a love to baptize
we're a ship set to capsize
into the inevitable sunrise.

a light sway with
sun rays on a Friday
can i make you mine,
right here, on our day?

beachside blanket &
eggs in a basket,
to you i deliver
my heart in a casket.

untitled.81318

i touch you behind tinted windows
my fingertips sing in crescendo

our hands go where the wind blows,
call this poem an innuendo

you say you love me
why don't you show me?

let's make some proof
under my sunroof

i crowned you czar,
just get in my car
let me take you far

untitled.10218/P2

heartbeat harmonics/
narcotic symphonic

you show me new tempos
that i keep as mementos

you turn lyrics into glory,
love songs to true stories.

your voice is a song
that i play night and day

if i make a playlist or two
can i sync my heart into you?

untitled.10218/P3

button down tucked in denim
your beauty stuns with venom
leather belts, slick back hair
you've got me saying prayers

cap on backwards, sleeves rolled up
i can't believe my dumb luck
your best kept secret, key and locket
but keep my hand in your back pocket

your shirt smells like new
wish it fit me like it fits you
but it's the same hue of
torch blue like my love for you

skin like marble, statue of David
every curve of you a home and a haven
lips like wine, red divine
moan and sigh and know you're mine

untitled.8118/P2

two princes, pale moonlight
clock strikes 12, we end at midnight

i don't want reason or rhyme
i need what's left of your time

no point in talking about it
what's said is to be done about it

just have my hand for our last dance,
a final flicker of summer romance...

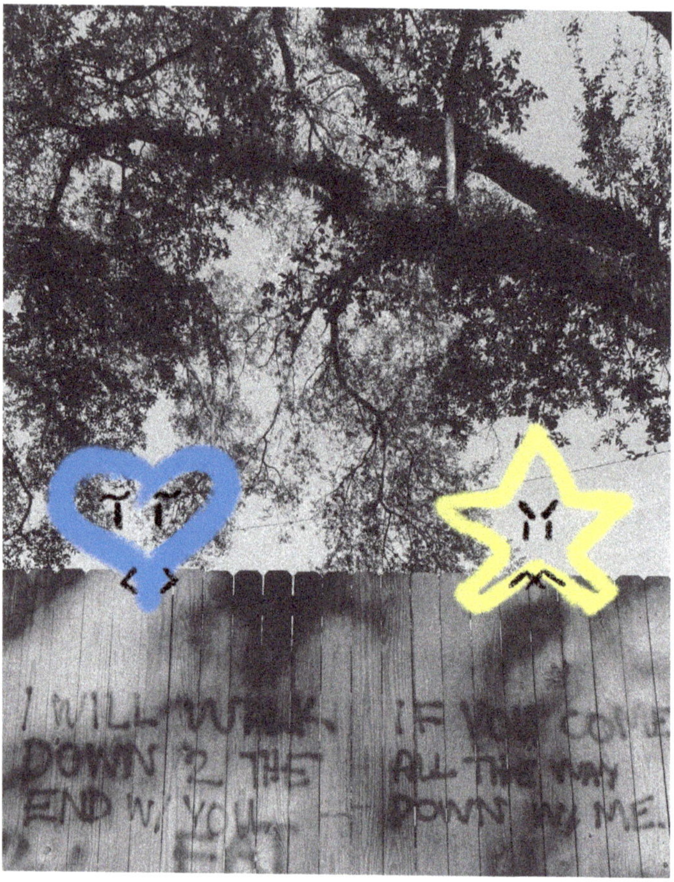
I WILL WALK
DOWN 2 THE
END W/ YOU
IF YOU COME
ALL THE WAY
DOWN W/ ME.

Dysclosure

i wonder when the time i act my age will come
because i'm too old now to be 'young and dumb'
but that's what i was when i jumped the gun
and put up that photo of him and i having fun..
just thinking about it makes my head run

i never said i'm sorry for being that way,
i don't know why i posted him that day
i should have given it time, let it breathe,
cause here i am now, clenching my teeth,
with the would haves/could haves at war in my sleep.

time has passed now, more than the length of us
and i texted you once since my thoughts don't rust
i didn't want closure or try to earn your trust,
i just wanted to know you were better off without
us and the doubt it might have brought about

about guys, about love, about all of the above
cause someone will be as lucky as i was to see what you're made of

thanks for showing me what i can do,

i know it won't hold a candle to the promise in you.

ben

you weren't supposed to be a part of this deal,

few weeks of dating isn't worth a rhyme

but you remind me of how much i can feel

in such a short amount of time.

Sk/eye/s

6' ft tall,
beard a shade of fall,

i hold my breath and count to ten;
i know you're a catch before i come in.

you almost touch me and i tense up
i touch you, let my heart fess up.

you kiss me in front of your window
and i want to learn your body's lingo.

my mind's a wreck with
your lips around my neck,

when you grab my hips
the way the sea holds ships.

you look at me with such intent,
do you know how you disorient?

you come over, stay a while.
how much can i make you smile?

2 past midnight, we touch and talk
you set your 7 AM alarm clock

you sink into slumber and
i can't help but wonder how

i want to see more of you...
what have i got myself into?

6 foot tall,
beard a shade of fall,
you're a blue eyed sirens call.

Bonbon Breeze

i can feel you next to my head..
i felt you open up like you did our bed.
i tried to focus on the book that i read
you didn't snore, you just moved me instead

i read your poem, you read some of mine
you asked me to be your Valentine
were we seeing the same signs?
we moved so fast in so little time

there was a lot going on, i understood
your school, your parents, you did all you could
i wanted to be there to keep you steady
but i understood you just weren't ready.

i guess, somewhere, there are two roads
and in the middle, they crash and fold
it's there we meet, so sugar sweet
a bonbon breeze, fleeting retreat

but there you were, face on my screen
you moved, you said; a life serene.
a second chance for a second dance,
you reached out and i grabbed your hands.

a drive away on a busy day,
still smiled & laughed like yesterday.
an hour together with no radio on
just you and me, our favorite song.

your blankets were home in your frozen abode
til you came back and gave me what you owed
all that time apart but you jumpstart my heart
with a night on your bed, a finished work of art.

sun comes up and so do we
and you tell me of your anxiety
i did what i could and understood
but from this came no good.

the first hour here we played fingertips
but the whole hour back was ellipse...

and just like that,

you paid for my ride, we said our goodbyes;
two ships leaving dock & to never pass by.

luke

i checked you out, you read me open
we started off on the same page
but i read fast, a few lines ahead
and with that you'd make your bed

i'd go back, pick up where we left,
i wanted to get through the end with you
and at some point, you did too
but now it was starting to feel like theft

back and forth was all we knew
but it was fun being your player two

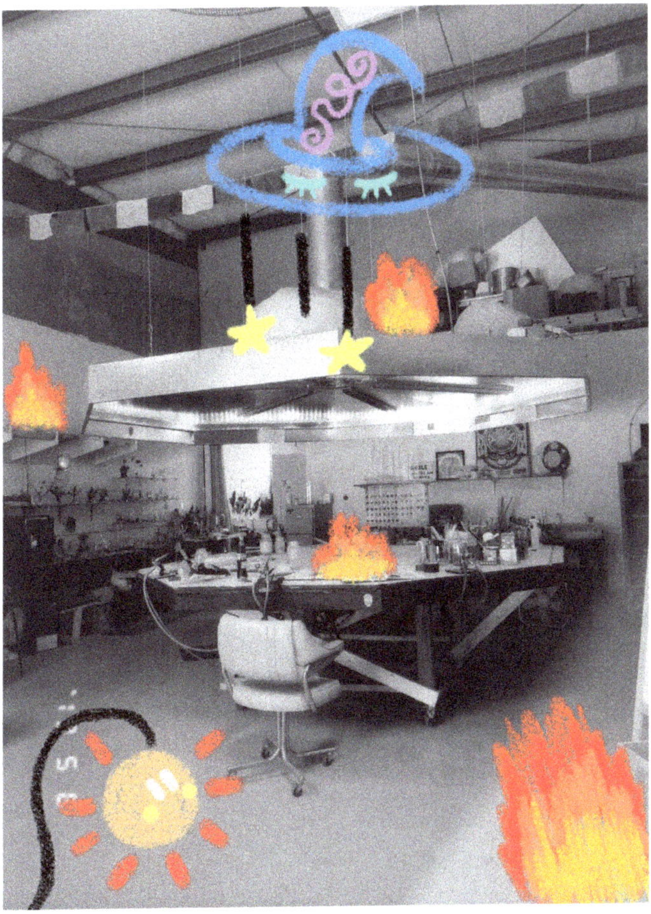

Californication

you'd pass by, leave some things behind
not so out of sight, barely out of mind

light brown eyes, a tattooed wonder
i fucking love your little blunders

how you trip on the table, fiddle with your shoes,
how you laugh when i kiss you playing the blues

we'd have some fun, fool around,
made my bed our playground

you'd come here once, maybe twice,
wouldn't play nice until it suffice

your humor's ironic, a smile iconic
you felt like the best kind of chronic

we went out one day to the art park
and from friction came first spark

you kissed my neck and held my hand
i lit up like a fanfare band

it was at Railroad Square where
i wanted you mine, then and there

but my days here were limited,
so goes this love inhibited

we enjoyed what's left, blind eye to the rest,
but i think i could have guessed..

i spent some time away and you still said "hey",
so i couldn't wait for the words i had to say

i wanted to make your day
so i made you a sock bouquet

when i said i'm here to stay, you turned me to clay
your smile the song of an orchestra play

"i'm glad you're staying", you say to me,
and i couldn't help but agree.

See You At the Bottom

you feel like free fall,

flurries of wind

but i see you above,

i can't quite get a hold of...

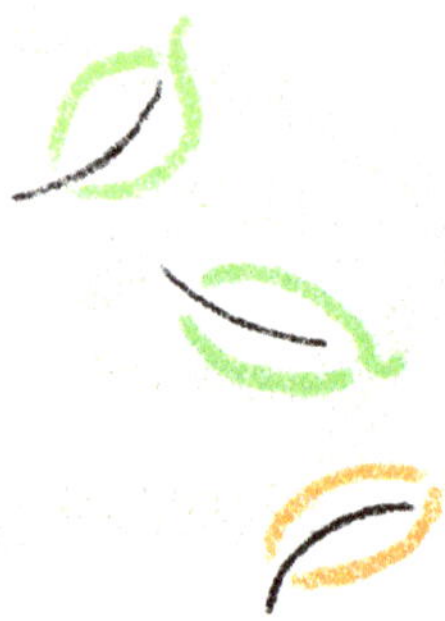

i feel you float,

a drift of grace,

like a leaf in autumn

i'll see you at the bottom.

i hope you don't mind that i left mine on the shores of Seaside.

Player Two

i like the sound of our title screen
a tranquil lullaby, colors serene
much like those farming RPGs
where fruit and joy bloom with ease

which save should we load,
the car rides on long roads,
or the one with the roaches we loathe?
we've got enough time for both.

you fuck me and my heart's on pause,
critical hit from the final boss.
a constant battle, who knows whose,
but I don't mind when I lose.

good thing i got luck in my skill tree,
that's how i got you in my inventory.
i love co-op but if you want i can fight you,
just about anything for my player two.

we were a bed too big in a tent too small.

trent

grade school crush
the flustered rush of recess
color block frolick
fake cigs and analog sticks

you took me back to elementary when
the boy i liked kicked my feet under the seat

TatamiMayday

do you think of me
like i think of you?

am i a seed in your memory
or the vapor of morning dew?

i read your daily affirmations
with concerning admiration
and wonder how the fuck did i get here.

i went to a farmers market and bought you a plant
i want to not think about you but i just can't
so i'll just stare at your gift on my nightstand.

i text you when i think about your pretty face
but i always wish i just pressed backspace

is it selfish of me that i want your within
when i have nothing but you to win?

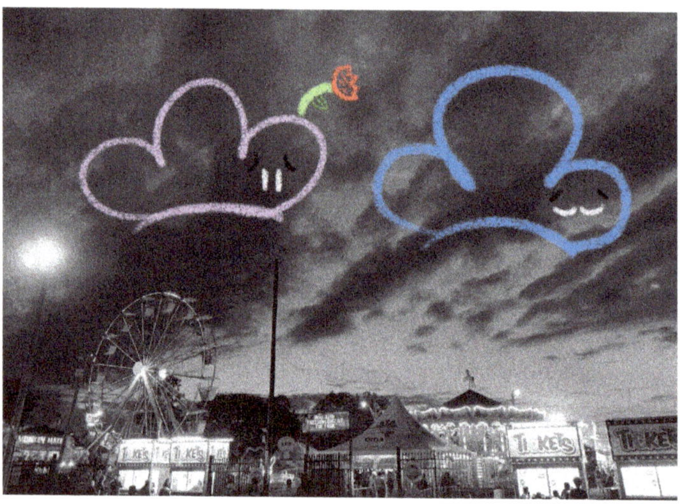

Autumn Sparks

the fire crackles avenues on its planes,
scorching veins along burning lanes

neon yellow-orange highlights
embers dance in full moonlight

crisp cracks of wooden timber
stored away for the coming winter

the flame lashes raging red ashes
pulse and glow like crimson snow

we talked about growing up
warming up in your backyard

i ease my breath and try to relax
any lapse i have when you hold my hand

a flickering candle along a wild blaze
your face puts me in some kinda haze

we have a good time, it's been pretty fun
can't wait to see how far you go in the long run

Tourist

if i climb up the staircase of you,
would you let me see the view?
i want to explore you on every floor,
can i see what's behind your closed doors?

i wonder if your walls are elegant,
royal with matching gold elements.
or are they white and minimal,
with hanging plants, faults invisible?

took a peek around, liked what i saw.
you're warm like home, you make winter thaw
met some of your friends, wanted to comprehend
the way you work, the way you mend.

but my visit was a short one,
i think i jumped the gun when
i told you how you make me feel
and maybe it was a big deal.

i don't know, but that's just it though
one can't always know where the wind blows
so along the way, it finds a spark...
could there be light or will it go dark?

a

l

o

n

g

f

a

l

l

makes your heartbeat stall.

alex

for some reason
the words for you are the hardest to write.
i'm not sure why,
it could be because i'm with you daily and
my pen works best when you can't distract me

they say
great art comes from misery
so,
maybe it's cause you make me happy?
(should I make this book less sappy?!)

here's the thing:
i could write about the others since
their stories had their endings written
ready to publish, send to print.
so in my opinion,
i think it's cause i don't want to jinx it.

a writer's nightmare is a work incomplete
or worse: CTRL+A+Delete
so i hope you know that this is my craft
but you're the only draft I don't want to finish.

i'm the apple of the corner of your eye

Paper Volcano

sink and swim all over your skin
smoke you in every time you grin

grow on me like clinging static,
explode in me like vertigo panic.

simmer and boil every time i come over
zero to hundred, don't go any slower

i like the heat of our chemistry,
we tend to ignite so breathlessly

you're like after-sex nicotine,
a sexual methamphetamine

my matter's reactive, your's combustible,
but i dig your fumes and i'm pretty adjustable.

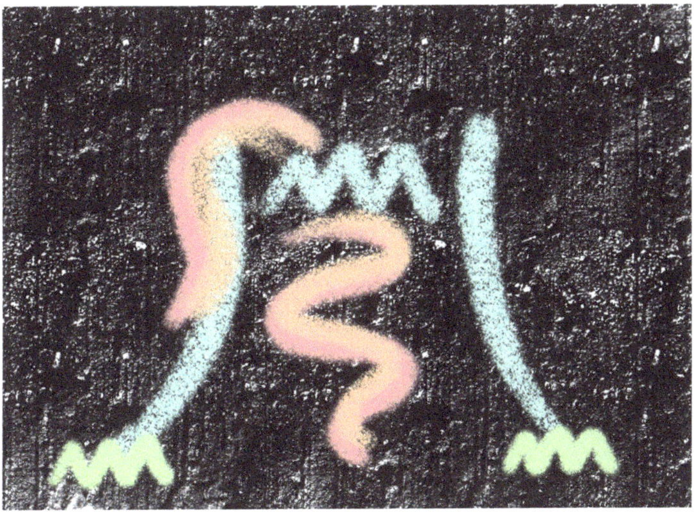

wild thing

it's all the little things with you

that make me feel light blue:

like that smirk you give me,

or how you grin like that one emoji 😬

the way you laugh with so much heart and

you talk so loud, it's my favorite part.

you call your mom and brother every day

just to say hi, make sure they're okay.

abrasive or assertive, can't ever tell but

get in your way and you're sure to raise hell.

you're so unworried, you live so free

and i like how you want to spend time with me.

i like that we have so much to say since

we already see each other every day,

i kid a lot about you getting tired of this but

there's nothing like finding hi's & goodbye's on your lips.

you can be crude, have an attitude sometimes,

yet here i am writing some poetry lines

about how i hate that you take up most of the bed

but i love all the other ways you get stuck in my head.

i love the way the lines of your fingerprints

follow mine behind your illegal tints,

and somewhere between me and your trash

you can hear the sound of my heart crash.

your smile always says to me, "eternity."

Dandelion

i want to tell myself to take a step back but
when you're in midair you can't really backtrack

i built up a friendship with nothing to fill it besides
good vibes, vague times, & quiet car rides

and frankly i don't know where to go from here
cause i don't think i can stop holding you dear

idk... i like dreaming about giving
every touch or look meaning

you feel like the first day of summer,
like the first flash of morning color.

you're like that crush from senior high who'd
smile my way and give me butterflies

you're a classic car with the top down
on a midnight highway with no one around.

but it didn't come without some kind of disappointment
you said you don't love me like some unholy anointment

i thought i was blooming a garden of flowers but
it's just a thicket of weeds I can't call ours.

i want to be more than just a memory
but it wouldn't stay true to your legacy...

but that's okay, i'm well aware of
the price i pay for the cost to care.

i'll just sit back and enjoy the ride
while i've still got time by your side.

Salt

season and spice,
bitter or nice,
too little, too much
but i'll love you as such.

sprinkle you over my shoulder,
like picking the luckiest clover.
you make life taste much bolder,
turn everything just a little bit golder.

you're the lull of my life

i found God in the mundane.

i see religion in routine,
heaven in the humdrum.

wisps of glitter float up
when i sweep the floor dust

there's grace in the laundry's swirl,
in the twirl of folding hands.

i taste divinity in his cooking
the lords of Cuban food overlooking

boring with you feels like freedom
so I built a home in our tedium.

i like doing nothing with you cause at least I'm doing something with you

Apt. 711

Light, thin cupboards
Smoked cherry wood
Timber-shaded neighborhood

Two-in-one laundry
Pastel pink Febreeze
The AC's set to 75 degrees

Black and white fittings
Pink and blue accents
$30 spent on our 4th of July "event"

Two fish tanks
Ten speed bumps
And an Oscar jump

Hand-me-down couch
Thrift store shopping
And credit card hopping

Off center window,
Some faulty stoves
Our home's a treasure trove

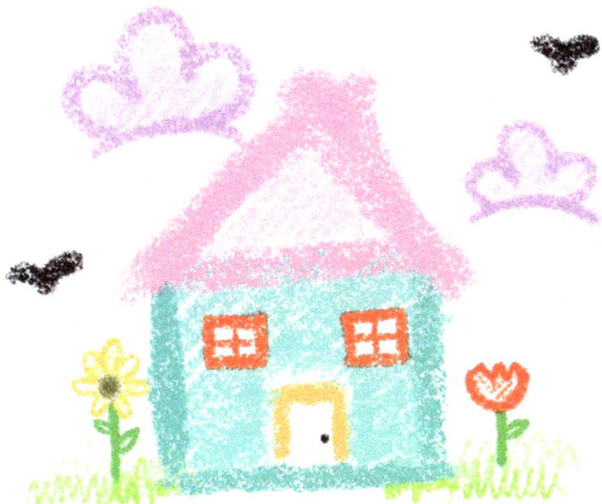

Home

King bed with some morning views
Eggs, bacon, and orange juice
White walls line the halls undressed
Consider my love professed

Red porch with a screen, green bubble serene
Mushrooms canopy the grass
Tree bark with squirrel-y remarks
But in time, this too shall pass

can i find abodes in places we don't own
in buildings borrowed for time,
or am i a nomad who's always at roam
since you're the home i call mine?

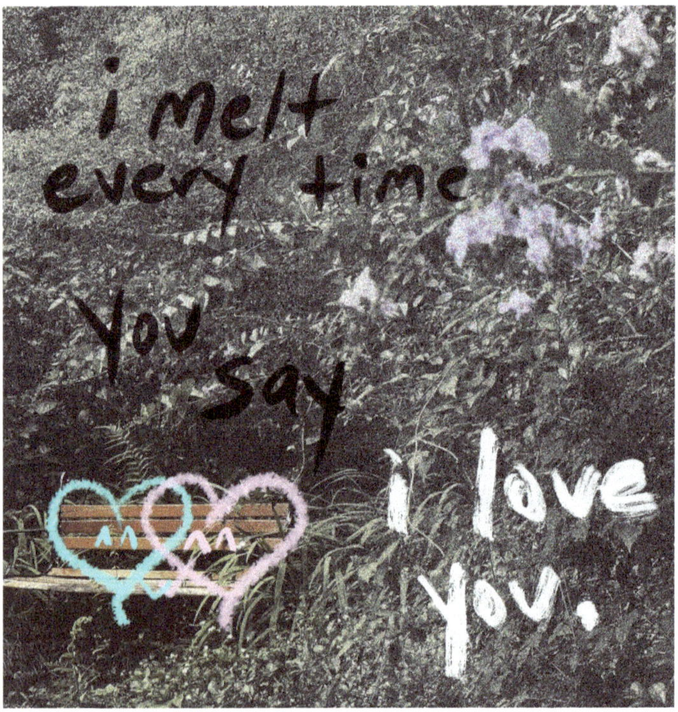
i melt
every time
you
say
i love
you.

outro.

before i leave you,

i wanted to say that it’s okay to love the way you do.

there’s no such thing as loving too much,

only when you don’t love yourself as such.

Acknowledgements

To all the boys I've liked/loved in this book,
I wonder what it's like to see your name in these pages.
Hope you don't mind.

Thank you Cami, Brigith, & Sigrid;
all those hours hearing me talk about boys and writing finally led to something!

Thank you Imogen Heap & Lana del Rey,
Your voices helped me find mine.

Thank you so much ***Alex****.*
You always surprise me with how much I can love you.
The way you love me always surprises me more though.
I'm sure I'll feel just like a boy when I watch you read this.
Here's to us. <3

Most of all,
Thank you ***boy blue****.*
See?
Told you you could do it.

www.ingramcontent.com/pod-product-compliance
Ingram Content Group UK Ltd.
Pitfield, Milton Keynes, MK11 3LW, UK
UKHW060116010826
14089UKWH00003B/12

9 781736 623909